This Book Belongs To

____

Made in the USA
Las Vegas, NV
07 December 2024

13536800R00063